Apprehensions of Van Gogh

Selected Poems, 1960-2014

Apprehensions of Van Gogh

Selected Poems, 1960-2014

David Pratt

First Edition

Hidden Brook Press
www.HiddenBrookPress.com
writers@HiddenBrookPress.com

Copyright © 2015 Hidden Brook Press
Copyright © 2015 David Pratt

All rights for poems revert to the author. All rights for book, layout and design remain with Hidden Brook Press. No part of this book may be reproduced except by a reviewer who may quote brief passages in a review. The use of any part of this publication reproduced, transmitted in any form or by any means, electronic, mechanical, photocopied, recorded or otherwise stored in a retrieval system without prior written consent of the publisher is an infringement of the copyright law.

Apprehensions of Van Gogh: Selected Poems, 1960 – 2014
by David Pratt

Editor – Bruce Kauffman
Cover Design – Richard M. Grove
Layout and Design – Richard M. Grove

Typeset in Garamond
Printed and bound in USA

Library and Archives Canada Cataloguing in Publication

Pratt, David, 1939-
[Poems. Selections]
    Apprehensions of Van Gogh : selected poems, 1960-2014 / David Pratt.

ISBN 978-1-927725-21-4 (paperback)

    I. Title.

PS8581.R375A6 2015   C811'.54   C2015-904188-0

For Kathy, Rosemary, and Jonathan

Acknowledgements

I wish to express my thanks to the editors of the literary journals in which many of the poems in this collection first appeared.

I also wish to thank Bruce Kauffman for his meticulous editing, which did much to improve the text, and the publisher of Hidden Brook Press, Richard M. Grove, who had immediate faith in the manuscript sent to him by an obscure poet.

Above all, I am indebted to the persons and places that gave rise to these poems, and enriched my life.

Contents

To Hell with It – *p. 3*
Irving Layton Reads – *p. 4*
Fred Varley in His Studio – *p. 5*
Louis Germain – *p. 6*
The Dancer – *p. 7*
Checkout – *p. 8*
La Herradura – *p. 9*
A Hospital in Spain – *p. 10*
When Seasons Change – *p. 11*
Spring Break in Hania – *p. 12*
End of Summer – *p. 13*
On Wolfe Island – *p. 14*
Snow Angel – *p. 15*
The Ice Was Singing – *p. 16*
Winter Evening, Chemong Lake – *p. 17*
Five Haiku for Iphigenia – *p. 18*
Last Day on Skyros – *p. 19*
Every Night I Go Back to Skopelos – *p. 20*
The Cretan Runner – *p. 21*
Aegean Wind – *p. 22*
Ancient Doors – *p. 23*
Siesta – *p. 24*
Taverna Omeros – *p. 25*
Home – *p. 26*
A Ballad of General Maud'huy – *p. 28*
Karl Ludwig's Night Out – *p. 30*
The Death of John Pendlebury – *p. 32*
Partisans – *p. 33*
The Hero – *p. 34*
Rescue at Cabanatuan – *p. 36*
Reflections – *p. 38*
Aubade – *p. 39*
Parting – *p. 40*
A Kind of Lightness – *p. 41*

Road Kill – *p. 42*
André Frenaud – *p. 43*
Al Purdy at the Young Socialist Forum – *p. 44*
Elizabeth Barrett Browning Dies in Florence – *p. 45*
Maria Kalogeropoulos – *p. 46*
Boulevard St. Germain – *p. 47*
I Have Come Here to Forget – *p. 48*
Ivan Ivanovich Ozolin – *p. 49*
George Gabori Recalls His Comrades – *p. 50*
August 1968 – *p. 51*
Red Snow – *p. 53*
Chen Tsao-Fen – *p. 55*
Isaac Babel – *p. 56*
Hideki Yukawa – *p. 57*
Marie Curie at the Front – *p. 58*
Nocturne – *p. 60*
The Dead Child by Jakub Schikaneder – *p. 61*
Edvard Munch: The Sick Child – *p. 62*
The Sculptor of Conques – *p. 63*
Builders of the Parthenon – *p. 65*
Daylight Saving – *p. 66*
Uncle Jake – *p. 67*
Exemptions – *p. 68*
At Street Corners – *p. 69*
Odysseus and the Siren – *p. 70*
I Am the King Your Father – *p. 72*
Sweet Wells – *p. 73*
In Nopigia – *p. 74*
Grandfather – *p. 75*
On a Cuban Street – *p. 76*
Plaza Vieja, Havana – *p. 77*
Hotel du Cygne – *p. 78*
In the Uffizi – *p. 79*
King David's Spring – *p. 80*
The Potter's Husband – *p. 81*
The Poems of Judith Pond – *p. 82*

The Abersychan Writers Group – *p. 83*
Kari Leaves Home – *p. 84*
Leaving Palm Springs – *p. 85*
After an Absence – *p. 86*
Part of a Biography of a Garden – *p. 87*
Prairie Graveyard – *p. 88*
Voyageur – *p. 90*
Missionaries – *p. 91*
Sheep Market – *p. 92*
I Am Cooking Jambalaya – *p. 94*
Finishing Touches – *p. 95*
Moments – *p. 96*
The Gift That's Unexpected – *p. 97*
Vanishing Point – *p. 98*
Doubt – *p. 99*
Lazarus – *p. 100*
Old Miner – *p. 101*
A Good Death – *p. 102*
Poodle – *p. 103*
Potiphar's Wife – *p. 104*
The Canopic Jars – *p. 105*
Tango Lesson – *p. 106*
Sebastian – *p. 107*
Yes, We Had Comrades – *p. 108*
Apprehensions of Van Gogh – *p. 110*

Author Bio – *p. 60*

Preface

When Joseph Brodsky was on trial in Leningrad in 1963 on a charge of social parasitism, he argued that he was not a parasite but a poet. What educational qualifications do you have, the judge asked, to entitle you to call yourself a poet? "I don't think poetry comes from an education," Brodsky answered. "I think it comes from God." He was sentenced to five years hard labour.

Few poets today would claim so candidly to be touched by divine fire. Nevertheless, there is an ineffable quality in poetry that, as in music, dance, painting, sculpture, and the other arts, distinguishes it from the prosaic. For one thing, poetry has an element of the physical, of eros, of earth, fire, and water. And the truest responses to poetry are physical: goose flesh, laughter, and tears. For me, the meeting place of form and substance is also the rendezvous of the mind and heart. A poem is not simply an intellectual exercise; I can write only of matters about which I care deeply. Alex Colville expressed this eloquently:

> I once said that I painted people and animals which are wholly good. I was really saying that the element of love, of deep attachment, of ascribing unqualified significance to particular living beings (which are in a sense inventions) and above all of feeling that there is transcending importance in certain relationships of elements—this element is central in the process of making art.

This collection contains most of the poems, written over five decades, that I would like to preserve. The poems come in three forms: formal poems, non-formal poems, and prose poems. In my experience, the form of the poem emerges naturally from the substance. I confess that I have never been much influenced by contemporary trends. Fashion has always seemed to me an emblem of superficiality, most of all in the arts.

The tradition I admire is lyrical and narrative, and runs back from such poets as Irving Layton and Dylan Thomas through Eliot and Frost, Housman and Tennyson, to Chaucer and Homer. In the twentieth century, this tradition bifurcated. One school became the academics of the avant-garde, the other the troubadours of popular songs. The middle ground of popular poetry was left virtually unoccupied. Newspapers stopped printing poems and reviewing poetry books. Today most poetry is published in subsidized journals produced by university English departments. In the public eye, the cultural traction of poetry has come close to that of macramé. As the Polish poet Wislawa Szymborska observed, "Bureaucrats and bus passengers respond with a touch of incredulity and alarm when they find that they're dealing with a poet."

The second law of thermodynamics posits that everything must decay, die, and vanish into its environment. Those who still write poetry do so in defiance of this law. If any of the poems in this collection provoke incredulity or alarm, their creation will not have been in vain.

Apprehensions of Van Gogh

To Hell with It

After staring at the unforgiving page all day,
seeking in vain the incandescent phrase,
I said to hell with it and went out to the lake.
Beavers and winter storms had brought down trees
across the trails; I cut them where they lay,
then threw the logs into a disused mica mine
that needed filling in. Old cedar trunks
clad in green slime, submerged a century,
rested in the shallow water of the bay;
I winched them out and stacked them up to dry.
I got three hundred seedlings of white pine
and sweated with a pickaxe and a spade
to plant them in the stubborn rock and clay.
Woodpeckers drummed, blackflies besieged my eyes,
geese in formations migrated overhead,
loons called and dived, a heron flapped away:
that was my poetry for the month of May.

Irving Layton Reads

Aggressive, egotistical, and vain,
you scorn your rivals and deride your friends;
your poems redolent with love and pain,
contemptuous of literary trends.

The literati will not take your part;
your poetry unfashionably records
the motives of the genitals and heart.
It's not the style to win the big awards.

Aging ungracefully and overweight,
disparaged by your smoother, younger peers,
you startle, dumbfound, and intoxicate
with every poem you pour into our ears.

And in the end it is your poetry, yours,
the people greet with tears and wild applause.

Fred Varley in His Studio

He stands at the easel in old age,
in his attic space,
cigarette stubs at his feet,
boots by the table, on it a jug of milk,
a slice of cheese folded in a hunk of bread
cut with a butcher knife,
books and drawings strewn around the place.

He has a genius for losing
clothes, jobs, homes, and women,
and for capturing the darkness
of the notch at the base
of a throat, a model cupping an apple
in her timeless palm
with meditative grace.

Out of his poverty he bequeaths us
the planes of a shoulder, a forehead, a trace
of green shadow around a seductive mouth.
The brown cord coat is flecked with paint,
the palette thumb-hole smooth with use,
but the blue eyes are still bright
and watchful in the creased and fractured face.

Louis Germain

In summer in Algiers, amid the scents
of honeysuckle and horse dung,
old men with medals and missing limbs
sit on benches in the shade.
Shutters are closed against the dust,
and boys shout as they swim
in the harbour's silky water and violent sun.

Such boys he teaches.
Coaxes, drills, lectures them,
beats them impartially,
nurtures their intelligence,
this obscure, devoted teacher
in this poor colonial town.

When, in midlife,
Albert Camus receives the Nobel Prize,
he writes to his old teacher: *But for you…*
And Louis Germain,
now long retired, writes back:
My dear child…

The Dancer

The name on the long list caught his eye;
then he remembered: he had seen her dance
once, in Berlin, at the Operahaus,
in 1931 or '32,
when he was nineteen, studying philosophy.
He recalled the elegance, the discipline,
the art that came from ignorance of compromise.
He took the megaphone from the Unteroffizier
and called her name. And then again.

From the line of naked beings
one stepped out. Unrecognizable.
Skeletal ribs and pelvis, shrunken
breasts and thighs, face furrowed, hair gray.
You are the dancer? Wide-eyed, she nodded.
"Dance," he said. She stared uncomprehendingly.
Gripping his riding crop, he said again,
more softly, "Dance."

She began to dance. Awkwardly.
Stumbling. And then as if remembering
the music, as if awakening,
dreaming, began to dance.
A vault, a grand jeté,
sweeping nearer to him,
tore his pistol from the holster,
fired once, killing him instantly.
A storm of bullets cut her down.
The doors opened, and the line began to move.

Checkout

I load up with fresh salmon
and smoked oysters for this evening,
bacon and marmalade, optimistically,
checking my list, making tight turns
round the end of aisles,
and am brought up sharp behind drab clothes
untidy grey hair, cart blocking the aisle,
reading through thick glasses
the labels on cans. I say thank you curtly
when she notices and lets me by.

I pass cabbages and watermelons
stacked like heavy ordnance,
pick ears of corn, two avocados,
head for the checkout
and am behind her again
unloading sardines and day-old bread.

Impatiently, I observe
"Man Aged 91 Gives Birth to Twins;"
"John Kennedy Is Found Alive On Mars."

Fumbling with age-spotted hands in a plastic purse,
she counts out nickels, dimes,
searches for pennies (I exhale audibly),
holds out the coins in her palm
and I see, appalled:
the blue numbers tattooed on her wrist.

La Herradura

Wave after wave rolls into the horseshoe bay. The evening breeze stirs laundry on a rooftop, sifts through the orange trees, rattles the shutters of condos closed for winter. In waterfront cafés, sleek German tourists drink beer and watch the sunset. I follow boot prints in the darkening sand.

Wave after wave of Moroccan troops. The guns, and then the knives. Men of good will fell back, and fell. Just beyond the breakers, a fisherman rests his oars and pays out net. Shadows invade the village, colour migrates from earth to sky. Cafés switch on blue lights.

Wave after wave of civilians fleeing the wreck of Malaga. Ambulances try to forge a path. Mothers beg the drivers to take their babies. The sea is a dangerous green tonight. The setting sun begins to ignite the sky.

Wave after wave of bombers of the Condor Legion, blasting holes in the crowds of refugees. On the beach, a man stands behind a woman, his arms around her waist as they look out to sea. The ruined tower on the headland is now a silhouette.

Wave after wave of arrests and executions. There are no memorials. Behind the town a shrouded moon rises above the hills. The dying sun gashes a wound in the horizon. The fronds of palm trees whisper, and are still. The boot prints in the sand are filled with blood.

A Hospital in Spain

I can feel each finger, bend each one,
but my hands will not again caress a woman's breasts.
They've taken out one eye. I'm blind.
The smell. The cries. The many languages.
Ten days ago, I was in Sweden, on the farm.
The shell blew off one hand, the surgeon took the other.
I am so cold. So weak. Clothes, skin of my face,
all stiff with blood. A voice close to my ear: a Dane.
"You need blood," he says. "The Canadian doctor, Beth,
will give you blood." While they warm the blood
I try to say it was my first engagement,
old rifles against tanks and flamethrowers.
I'm useless to my comrades now;
I have done nothing to advance the cause.
A swab on my forearm, smell of iodine, the needle.
The coldness goes. I feel the pumping of my heart again.
The Dane speaks as they leave: "The doctor says
you will see again with your good eye."
And as for women: I still have my lips.

When Seasons Change

When seasons change, the currents are profound.
Our boots crunch through the brittle crust of ice;
We sense the spring arriving underground.

Late winter snow has eiderdowned
the jagged spurs of granite and of gneiss.
When seasons change, the currents are profound.

We stop, unspeaking, and the only sound
is dead leaves skittering like mice.
We sense the spring arriving underground.

Last night I watched you sleeping and I found
your classic face, for once, did not entice.
When seasons change, the currents are profound.

I think you must have dreamed, because you frowned
and murmured indistinctly once or twice.
I sense the spring arriving underground.

These woods will not much longer be snowbound;
a tide of sap flows north beneath the ice.
When seasons change, the currents are profound.
We sense the spring arriving underground.

Spring Break in Hania

The harbour bars are swarming with a throng
of teenagers who've come from northern Greece;
they whistle, dance, and argue all night long,
drink on the sidewalks and ignore the police.

These streets and squares I hardly recognize.
I squeeze along a crowded alleyway,
to find these children have monopolized
all tables in my favorite café.

But suddenly I shiver as it seems
a company of ghosts confronts my eyes,
gray-headed people who have lost their dreams,
worn down with work and grief and compromise.

My scowl evaporates. Let youth delay
the debts that time incurs, and age must pay.

End of Summer

It is so abrupt, the end of summer,
the August water soft for swimming,
droplets sparkling from the paddle blade,
then suddenly the maples blaze ahead
like stop lights; it's September,
you're a year older, and once again,
the dreams of June are unfulfilled.

You look up, as you take out the garbage,
or pee off the deck,
at a serious moon, a billion stars,
sniff the wind for frost,
turn inward, prepare for ice,
prepare to walk on water.

But sometimes, when you hear
a random skein of geese invisible in the dark,
or see them as a distant line of smoke,
your heart swivels like a compass needle
seeking south. Beavers are cutting birches.
You shiver in the damp air,
bring in more logs, steel yourself for winter,
your adversary and your home.

Snow Angel

Nine choirs of angels,
form three hierarchies:
the seraphim, cherubim, and thrones;
the dominions, virtues, and powers,
the principalities, archangels, and angels.
So wrote Dionysius
the Areopagite.

"I would lie for hours in the snow,
waiting for someone to come
so I could get up
without spoiling my angel.
If there are five or six of you,
you can make a circle of angels;
but someone has to stay outside
to help you out."

Aquinas tell us that the fallen angels
fell due to their envy of man.
Angels, he averred, have neither

extension nor dimension,
they consist of form and matter,
but the latter is not corporeal;
several angels may occupy the same space.

Before you freeze to death in your angelic circle,
take my corporeal human hand.
Let us occupy the same space,
and make angels and archangels,
principalities, dominions, virtues, powers,
seraphim, cherubim, and thrones
envy us
and fall.

The Ice Was Singing

Dear Heart, Yesterday the lake was snow-free
and smooth as a ballroom floor.
A family of deer moved back among the trees,
turning to look at me.
The ice on the lake was singing.
A porcupine climbed slowly down
from the branch where it was feeding
and galloped away, ungainly as a cow.
Beavers must have cut the line to the raft;
it had drifted a long way down the shore
before it froze in.
How are you, and your husband,
and your baby?
The oak tree I gave you is four feet high.
The ice was singing like a whale.

To Love Imperfectly

The lock is stiff
and the house smells of emptiness.

We chose this place for its white walls
and its simplicity.

I climb the steep stairs up which I brought you
coffee and flowers each morning.

The bedroom seems larger
without the bed.

What eluded us here was laughter
and either of us saying yes! yes!

I vacuum carpets. The machine coughs
and spits. Perhaps a paperclip.

I stoop to pick it up, and find a bent and broken
earring of silver filigree.

To love imperfectly
is to grieve completely.

Winter Evening, Chemong Lake

Blue shadows mark the snow with the approach of night.
Your room is prismed with the sun's last rays.
Your hair upon the pillow's streaked with light.

Beside the dock our skis still stand upright,
the tracks we made recede into the haze.
Blue shadows mark the snow with the approach of night.

Your face beneath the quilt is out of sight,
but the sunset through the willow tree displays
your hair upon the pillow streaked with light.

Your house is spare and clean, austere and bright;
your golden dog lies by the wood stove's blaze,
blue shadows mark the snow with the approach of night.

At this one moment, everything is right.
I listen to your breathing as I stand and gaze
at your hair upon the pillow streaked with light.

Words flow like wounds. I seek the perfect phrase
to paint your nightdress on the floor, to praise
your hair upon the pillow streaked with light,
in the gold and silver shadows of this midwinter night.

Five Haiku for Iphigenia

Iphigenia
my black haired teacher of Greek:
the seaside café.

She feels the cool breeze
I hand over my sweater:
lemon blossom scent.

A wave breaks on the rocks
the spray almost reaches us:
this is our last time.

You are very kind
do not say thank you thank you:
I really mean it.

She writes with head bowed
in the book that she gave me:
two silver hairs gleam.

Last Day on Skyros

A blue line, to keep the devil out
around the house and terrace where we stand;
in the dark, we smell the wine-dark sea.
The drunken taxi drivers are asleep.
The dancers are asleep.
The dogs, the donkeys, the roosters are asleep.
The church bells are asleep.

We have left it too late.
"Are you afraid of your tenderness?" she asks.
No, it is rather that I have slept
too long and was dazed by the sun
and by her long lithe body
striding naked down the beach
burned the same copper as her hair.

My pack is full. I have thrown away
the goat skull with its curved satanic horns
I found in the middle of the island.
My boat leaves at dawn.

From the pines on the hillside
beyond the monastery where yesterday
we walked to the tiny frescoed chapel
comes a breeze
heavy with resin.

Every Night I Go Back to Skopelos

My brother was killed in Northern Greece
fighting the Italians in the snow.
When the war ended, we rejoiced, although
there was no work, and very little peace.

My husband said we'd emigrate. But I said no.
And then our youngest child, the baby, died.
On the dock, my mother screamed and cried.
We came to Canada, to Ontario.

It's April. I see the island in my sleep,
her flowers like waterfalls. I just don't know
how it can still be twenty-five below,
with drifts along the driveway four feet deep.

I'm thirty-three. I look like an old crow,
dressed head to foot in black, against the snow.

The Cretan Runner

We take the new road through the mountains to Agia Gonia. In the village square, children play round the war memorial. Outside the taverna three men sit at a table. Two wear the ragged clothes of shepherds, but the third is dressed in jet-black turban, baggy pants, high gleaming boots. Under the aquiline nose, the cropped beard is silver. A shepherd's crook rests by his chair.

Leigh Fermor once asked a brigand, if he happened to find a man's wallet, whether he would keep it. "No," the brigand said, "That would be theft. It would be dishonourable. I would return it to the man. Then I would take it from him by force."

"Greetings, sirs," I say. "I am the Canadian." I gesture toward Ron. "This my friend is also the Canadian." I hold out my copy of The Cretan Runner. "I seek Georgiou Psychoundakis." The brigand takes the book from my hand. He turns to the photographs, recognizes people, grunts, shows the pictures to his friends. "Georgiou lives in Haniá now," he says.

But what I want to say is this: "Tell me about Georgiou Psychoundakis of Agia Gonia, the slight, modest man, who ran fifty miles a day through the mountains taking messages from cave to hideout, from transmitter to submarine, outflanking and outfacing Germans, risking every day a terrible death, leaving for his family only his small flock of goats, which others stole while he was away. Psychoundakis, who, after the war, by some bureaucratic bungle in Athens, was imprisoned for two years as a deserter, causing him such grief that all his hair fell out. Psychoundakis, who ended his working life caring for the graves in the German military cemetery. I have come to honor this man."

But my Greek is just not good enough.

Aegean Wind

A rooster crows. Then another.
And then a chorus. A donkey brays.
I turn on the light. It's 2:00 AM.
The wind has risen; a shutter bangs.
I step out on the rooftop and begin
to take my laundry off the line.
A cuticle of moon above the ruined fort
illuminates white houses
tumbling down the hill like sugar cubes.
Was it the wind that woke me,
or was it what she said today?

"When we traveled the road to Peshawar
we had to drive on the left;
when he couldn't see the road ahead
he would say, 'You are my eyes.'
It's hard, remembering this
because when they killed him
they also shot him through the eyes."

The wind is from the east,
and from the east no sign of light.
A dog begins to bark. A rooster crows.
I will not sleep again tonight.

Ancient Doors

Bright sun through the vine leaves
overhead; bunches of still-tiny grapes;
I watch a white cloud sliding past.

At the next table, three old men
with straw hats and shepherds' crooks
talk, laugh, click worry beads.

Down the middle of the cobbled street
on long tanned legs
she walks alone.

Ancient doors, blue shutters closing
for siesta, the whole village settling
into the dense shadows of two o'clock.

I'll ask her to come with me tonight
to see the greenness of the grapes
against the darkening sky.

Siesta

The turquoise shutters closed
against the blinding sky and sea,
the bleating of the goats,
and the raining blossoms of the Judas tree.

Her sleeping head rests on her arm,
line of the neck, shoulder, calf, articulate and tanned.
Her hair is tousled, burned tawny by the sun;
a ring glows silver on the upraised hand.

This morning on a wall in Cnossos,
we saw the image of a charging bull,
his massive shoulders hunched
and ivory horns outthrust;
snorting, head down, the bull, the Bull of Minos
eyes bulging, hooves pounding
in the powdered Cretan dust.

Taverna Omeros

A breeze from the sea
rustles the roof of vine leaves,
your burgundy shirt whispers
against your skin.

The white broken line of waves
where we walked
in the soft sand;
against the evening
the huge cliff;
under it
the lights of Skyros
pierce one by one the blue dusk.

A bowl of olives
on the checked table cloth;
this candlelit moment
you break bread, I pour wine,
this timeless first time
we take
eat
and drink
from the same glass.

Home

Skinny, we called him, because his name
was Skinner; and he suited it. Eighteen,
but scarcely five foot six, and bronchial,
gray-faced, you could tell green fields
had no part in his history.
How he got through the medical—
but this was 1917, when the "Passed A-1"
was a death certificate good for a month or two.

He never knew his parents,
and the staging camp at Arras
was one more orphanage to him.
For all their bellowing,
the NCO's left you alone at night.
But the winter damp was awful. Last in line
for evening medical parade, he heard the bugle
sound Lights Out before the drunk MO
gave him two sulfur tablets for his racking cough.

No moon, no lights. Hundreds of tents,
pale white, identical, row after row.
Searching in vain for some familiar point,
he opened a tent flap, was cursed by sleeping men,
stumbled through freezing mud,
tripped on guy lines, tried another tent,
was struck by boots thrown at his head.
And so he trod for hours this path of sorrows
till by some chance came where we were.

Through our fitful sleep and troubled dreams
we heard him stagger in and fall upon his pallet;
and then, and through the night,
again and again, we heard him groan,
before he slept, and in his sleep,
"I'm home. I'm home. I'm home."

A Ballad of General Maud'huy

The year was 1917,
the place was Northern France,
the Germans from their concrete lines
had halted our advance,
and we all thought who marched and fought
we lived by grace or chance.

A troop of twelve came down the road
as the sun began to rise,
an unarmed soldier in their midst
with terror in his eyes:
this was, by God, the firing squad
we'd come to recognize.

The General heard them going by
with steady sombre tread.
He stepped outside, held up his hand
and faced the man they led.
"What did you do?" he asked the youth.
"I left my post," he said.

"You understand you let us down?"
the General asked the man,
"We're ordering our troops to do
more than most mortals can;
we'd soon be done if everyone
threw down his gun and ran."

The soldier hung his head in shame,
but the General wasn't done.
"The example that we make of you
is an important one.
It means your pain is not in vain;
you die for France, my son."

The young man raised his lowered head,
his stance no longer cowed,
he now saw reason in his death
and stood with head unbowed.
His youthful face bore sorrow's trace
but now his look was proud.

The General shook the soldier's hand,
saluted a farewell.
A volley from a mile away
marked where our comrade fell.
The General lit a cigarette
and damned all wars to hell.

Karl Ludwig's Night Out

They still tell tales in the south of Wales
of a March night cold and damp
In wartime when some seventy men
broke out of prison camp.
They raised the alarm at Island Farm,
near Bridgend, Monmouthshire,
Where Karl Ludwig had helped to dig
the tunnel under the wire.

This SS man had a plausible plan,
as soon as he was free,
To jump, with luck, on a passing truck,
and make it to the sea.
But no trucks came, so his second aim
was to hop aboard a train;
Down Railway Street with stealthy feet
he hurried through the rain.

But on up ahead he heard the tread
of an elderly English male;
He'd been at the pub, where he'd had some grub
and a gallon of English ale.
Karl didn't wait, he slipped through a gate
and hid himself in a yard;
He managed to push right into a bush
and crouched there on his guard.

But this modest pile was the domicile
of the fellow of whom we speak;
As he entered his garden—I do beg your pardon—
he stopped to take a leak.
He left unaware of what he'd done there.
For since Hitler's war began
Every British guy would have given one eye
to have pissed on an SS man!

The Death of John Pendlebury

It's safer to go forward than retreat,
better face danger than take flight;
to leap, and then land lightly on the feet.

I told the General, if you arm the men of Crete,
no Nazi thug will see tomorrow's light;
it's safer to go forward than retreat.

Honour required of every young athlete
who faced the charging bull, to stand upright,
to leap, and then land lightly on the feet.

Go to the tavernas, go out and meet
old men who fought the Turks, who know in any fight
it's safer to go forward than retreat.

I'll not live now to see this sad defeat
by Hitler Youth prepared by day or night
to leap, and then land lightly on the feet.

I shot three paratroopers in the street,
but now against this wall my blood runs bright.
It's safer to go forward than retreat.
I'll leap, and then land lightly on my feet.

Partisans

From a Story by Primo Levi

The first warm day of spring in Byelorussia.
They stacked their weapons on the bank,
and bathed in the Gorin, shouting and splashing,
men and women, naked or almost.

Pavel brought his violin to the river bank
and a song began. Ten times as many
had come and gone. Each one brave,
each resourceful, each hoping to reach home again.

Let them be remembered: Jozek and Gedaley,
Venjamin and Lefka, Mendel and Edek.
The sentry died before he could raise the alarm.
The white bodies lay in the water or at the edge,
the stain of red drifting casually downstream.

The Hero

They asked the questions without much interest,
but with some impatience, the captain
already late for dinner with his family.
He shook his head each time,
knowing what was coming, he shook his head
and said through broken teeth, "To hell with you."
They expected this. Clipped the electrodes
one to a nipple, one to his penis, asked again,
then pressed the switch. His scream filled the room.
This was something new, beyond the possible.
Ten feet overhead,
pedestrians walked dogs, mailed letters.

Could anything be worse? It could be, and it was.
They raised the voltage.
His bowels emptied. His vomit hit the wall.
He was no longer screaming,
he was being screamed.
He still said "No!"

Listen now! At this point, he was a hero!
Had they stopped then,
ships, schools, and streets
would have been named for him;
medals, speeches, women smiling
through their tears.
But they didn't stop. They knew—
they were professionals,
and it was their job to know—
that everybody has a breaking point.
He drew on everything he had,
and everything was not enough.
It needed only five more minutes,
then they took him away on a stretcher.

And he survived. Stripped of his pension,
decorations, shunned by old comrades,
despised by those most frightened of their fear.
Became a school teacher, let's say, bought a dog,
didn't sleep much. Never quite sure again.
And never to receive
this posthumous homage
this inadequate belated praise.

Rescue at Cabernatuan

MacArthur did return, wading ashore
at Leyte, in October '44.
In January, his forces reached Luzon,
four separate landings aimed to execute
a pincer movement on the capital.
North of Manila lay the prison camp
of Cabernatuan. Most healthy men
had been dispatched as labor to Japan;
the camp held just five hundred officers
including doctors, amputees, and those
too sick to be shipped out. The army knew
the fate these could expect as it advanced.
While Philippine guerillas blocked the roads
against attack on each side of the camp,
one hundred twenty Rangers walked two days
beyond their lines. At dusk, they stealthily
crept to the camp perimeter, and opened fire.
The guards were cut to pieces. Rangers burst
into the barrack huts. "We're Yanks!" they yelled,
"You're free! Head for the gate!" The prisoners, sick,
confused, as pale as ghosts, stunned by the noise,
night-blinded from the lack of vitamins,
thinking this was the massacre they'd feared,
ran round in circles, and hid under beds.
The Rangers looked like giants, carrying
strange guns, with unfamiliar uniforms.
They picked the prisoners up, many of them
just skin and bones, not more than eighty pounds,
and carried them. The truth began to dawn.
"Thank you! Thank you!" They sobbed.
"Thank God you've come!
We thought the US had forgotten us."

With bullets humming overhead
the freed men headed out, the weaker ones
were borne in farm carts pulled by buffaloes.
The Rangers passed out smokes, ripped up their shirts
for bandages, gave barefoot men their boots.
"We thought that they were gods," one prisoner said.
Their liberation gave the sick new strength,
and, singing as they went, some marched all night.

Then trucks and army ambulances came
from the advancing lines to carry them.
Crowds of GIs stood by the road to cheer.
They passed a tank flying the Stars and Stripes
and struggled to their feet, to the salute,
and wept from open hearts, and without shame.

Reflections

The wind throbs like a wound.
The street lights sway.
Rain-soaked reflections tremble,
and the silence under concrete bridges
echoes with the words we didn't say.

Yes, I have eyes, but only for the road.
I recognize this route and where it goes.
It's not as simple as a single interchange.
I hear a far-off siren die away.

On cloudy nights like these
it's all the turnings that you didn't take
that crush the heart.
It's not the distance or the rainy skies
but the one-way streets of time
that make your body ache.

That's how it is for hours. I try all night to find
reflections of your lips your hair
your skin your eyes through the side streets
and the high roads and the freeways
of the country of my mind.

Aubade

Slept apart again last night. Half awake
I stumble against the coffee table
and knock your Bible to the floor.
Open the blinds, step out on the balcony;
the tide is in. In close formation
small waves advance.
From somewhere on the water come
disjointed cries of geese.
Patches of snow and cloud on the mountain tops.
On an island in the bay, individual trees emerge
against a strip of orange sky:
another wasted dawn.

Parting

The riderless horse
canters over the plain.

A Kind of Lightness

The dog was more startled
by my yell than by the crash
as the three wine glasses
went down like dominoes.

But as I swept up the fragments
I noticed that my mood
was not so much of sadness or chagrin
as a kind of lightness. Three glasses fewer,
now, to crowd the cupboard;
another step toward austerity.
And I recalled my mother,
moving to a smaller house,
then an apartment, releasing possessions,
and finally just the few books
and photographs beside the bed.

And this made me think of that final
talk with you last month.
How underneath the wintry rage
when finally I put down the phone,
pushed up an early crocus of relief.
I had resigned devotion, passion, hope,
just as I'd drop my pack as dusk came on
when I found the place to pitch my tent.
We give things up unwillingly,
and with thanks,
and that is how we die.

Road Kill

Along the dark road, I jog toward a darker shape:
a small carcass with tawny brindled tail,
lips frozen in a scream and mouth agape,
imploring paw out-thrust, palm creased and frail.

First death, then desecration. A later day:
a flock of crows crowds hungrily around
flesh chopped and pink, intestines blue and gray,
one listening ear still pressed against the ground.

Sullen in the bright days after rain,
I see at once what countless tires have done:
a strip of leather, a relic of past pain,
animal and its shadow becoming one.

In the end, I no longer notice. I just jog on.
That's how it was, after you'd gone.

André Frénaud

Last night at Shakespeare & Company,
a woman with a belt like a boxer's
read poems about torpedo juice
and psychotic vegetables;
she held her papers too near a candle,
and came close to destroying
a historic landmark
and a score of professional expatriates.

But here, in the Bibliothèque Nationale
is André Frénaud,
in the last months of his life;
André Frénaud, who wrote,
Haineusement mon amour, la poésie
and,
Où est mon pays? C'est dans la poème

An affable, elderly man,
he sits in the audience,
and listens to a panel discussing his work.

And when a latecomer asks,
why are we not hearing André Frénaud?
he stands and turns and blinks
through his glasses
and says

I'm no good at speaking in public,
but I am full of poems.

Al Purdy
at the Young Socialist Forum

The place is like a Sunday School,
hard chairs in rows, blankets for blinds,
a shelf with twenty titles by Leon Trotsky
and a poster saying Book of the Month:
The State and Revolution.

This was several years before I learned
that four of the five paid-up members
were working for the Mounties.

The Chairperson in a green skirt
reads her poems, followed by a big mustache
who reads his.
Purdy sits in the corner
smiling like Gary Cooper.

Three things saved that evening from nonentity:
I found a dime under my chair,
an old man came in late, with his dog,
and Al Purdy read his poems.

Elizabeth Barrett Browning Dies in Florence

As the procession passed, we bowed in veneration,
weeping for her like children who had lost their mother,
the champion of our cause, our longing for a nation;
we lined the streets, and comforted each other.

We wept for her like children who had lost their mother;
the beautiful English lady, loved by all;
we lined the streets, and comforted each other;
laurel and white flowers adorned her pall.

The beautiful English lady, loved by all,
a famous poet in her own land, we're told;
laurel and white flowers adorned her pall,
Signor Roberto's grief was tragic to behold.

A famous poet in her own land, we're told.
She kissed him a dozen times before she died.
Signor Roberto's grief was tragic to behold,
she had eloped with him from England as his bride.

She kissed him a dozen times before she died.
As the procession passed, we bowed in veneration.
She had eloped with him from England as his bride,
this champion of our cause, our longing for a nation.

Maria Kalogeropoulos

We Italians were not popular in Athens, but the Greeks at least preferred us to the Germans. I was walking down Patissiou Street, in the summer of 1941, eighteen, and very homesick. Suddenly, a heavenly voice, singing in Italian! It was the aria from the triumphal scene in Aida. And with what range, what passion! I was from Verona; what more need I say? A small crowd had gathered to listen, including some Nazi officers, although the Germans had forbidden noise in public. I looked up: a young woman, chunky, black-haired, intense, sat playing the piano and singing by a window. The name above the bell said Kalogeropoulos. At the end, she soared up an octave to an incredible E flat. Everyone burst into applause. I was yelling *Brava! Brava!* She came out on the balcony. *Grazie, grazie*, she said, looking at me with her enormous dark eyes. I went to her house the next day, taking some of my rations. After that, we met in the park, two or three times a week. She said she had been hungry ever since the war began. I brought food, and she would sing. That was Maria Callas. Before she became famous, before she became slim. All through that summer, until the war reached out and grabbed me once more in its bloody fist, the two of us, on the park bench, she singing, and I in tears, from the music, and for home.

Boulevard St. Germain

The pavement and the first bright leaves
of the plane trees were washed like a watercolour
as I walked past the statue of Danton,
and read the words on the pedestal:
"After bread, education
is the first need of the people."

I crossed the street and passed
a man on his knees,
holding a sign that said,
"Help me, please. I'm hungry."

When I realized what I'd seen, I went back
and put a coin in his hand.
He was about thirty. He wasn't kneeling down,
in comfortable meditation,
but kneeling up, like a medieval penitent.

Others can explain this.

I only know I dream with Danton
of a day when it's no longer possible
for a man to kneel in the street with a sign saying
      M'aidez
      SVP
      J'ai faim,
while another grown man
weeps useless bourgeois tears
all the way down Boulevard St. Germain.

I Have Come Here to Forget

Three times yesterday.
In the morning, on the rue des Ecoles,
near the Sorbonne,
your hair in a chignon, carrying a briefcase,
all in black except for your white face and hands
and the silver buckles on your shoes,
walking past the statue of Montaigne.

In the afternoon, on a bench
in the Place Charles Dullin.
A few inches taller, perhaps.
The trees overhead were just coming into leaf.
Pigeons plodded around your feet,
your bike was propped beside you,
your backpack on the ground.
You wore blue jeans and a brown leather jacket,
your legs outstretched disconsolately
at the edge of the sunshine, the light
catching your cheekbones, the breeze
blowing the hair back from your ears.

And then there you were again, late in the evening
with a silver-haired man, in the Métro,
standing with your back to me
as straight as a dancer. When more people
got on at the Champs Elysées
we were pressed together. I felt your warmth,
smelled your scent. Your head came up to my heart.
I looked down at the parting in your hair.

The twitch at the corner of my mouth
has started again.

Ivan Ivanovich Ozolin

Next to the Tsar, the most famous man in Russia,
next to none the most famous Russian in the world,
left his train at my tiny station, Astapovo,
on the line from Kozelsk to Rostov-on-the-Don
and asked for shelter.
Thin, stooped, and fevered, in flight from his family,
my wife and I immediately gave him the main room,
gave our bedroom to the rest of his party,
and crowded with our three children
into one bedroom. Reporters arrived
in their hundreds, with cameras,
then letters, flowers, telegrams, in their thousands.
Police, uniformed and plain-clothes,
mixed with the crowd, high-ranking ecclesiasts,
who were turned away, and crowds of peasants,
kneeling, crossed themselves,
and sang the hymn, Eternal Memory.
The wife arrived, by special train; he refused to see her.
A clutch of Moscow doctors uselessly attended him.
In his delirium, he muttered, "Seek, keep seeking."
I am a humble official, bald, bearded,
and bespectacled, but I had my day,
the day that Leo Nikolayevich Tolstoy
died in my station house.

George Gabori Recalls His Comrades

My political education started very young.
I was nineteen when I stood
under the showers at Dachau, waiting
to see whether water or gas would come out.

The People's Labor Camp at Reczk
was harder than Dachau.
Whenever I stood up, whenever I struck a guard
I did it for myself and for my fellow-prisoners
to give them the courage to stand up and survive.

I don't know how many days I spent
in solitary confinement. If you don't
engage in make-believe, play some kind
of spiritual game, you get crazy.

But night after night the poet George Faludy
recited his poems, gave us lectures
on history, on democracy.
All those who stood around his bunk
survived. His spirit—
we drank it like the thirsty man in the desert.

August 1968

When we rolled into Prague in our tanks,
we were welcomed with cheers and with thanks;
flags flew from their shops and their banks;
we put Dubcek and Cernik in chains.

Once the city had regained its calm,
we moved out with the motorized arm
and camped in the fields of a farm
on the Sasava River's green plains.

All my soldiers had come from afar,
from the east of the USSR,
some still worshipped the priest and the Czar,
and the hot blood ran fast in their veins.

Our rations were frugal and bland;
the men learned to live off the land;
a farmer, his hat in his hand,
complained about two of my men.

"They made off with my best pig," he said.
"They pointed their guns at my head
when I asked them to pay, and instead,
they butchered the pig there and then."

So I lined up my troops in review
and I asked him to pick out the two,
which he did without more ado,
where they stood in their ranks side by side.

"Are you certain?" I asked. "Yes," he said.
So I shot both the men through the head.
When the farmer saw them fall dead,
he passed out, he was so horrified.

When he rallied, his color was gray.
With an effort he managed to say,
"All I wanted was for them to pay."
"Well, now they have paid," I replied.

Red Snow

Twenty-eight below;
we were cutting birch that day,
in the waist-deep snow of Nuksha 2.
My brigade was led by one Pavlov, a criminal,
wolfbloods, they called themselves;
only one was a political,
and I was he,
I, Victor Herman, an American.

Those who lost hope died long ago.
Keep your axe sharp. Cut accurately.
Don't talk. Make your quota,
get your 400 grams of bread.

We're cutting near a railway line;
guards, with their dogs,
stand by the fire.
A small train comes into view,
clanks to a stop.

Soldiers jump out,
slide back a door, and the wagon
disgorges women, jumping, slipping,
falling in the snow, dirty, disheveled,
their faces white with fear and cold.
All are in summer dresses,
sandals and high heels, spring hats.
In what warm southern town
were these arrested?

We stand transfixed: it's years
since we have seen such creatures,
One, tall and pregnant,
stands apart. Team leader Pavlov
moves close to her.

"Listen, you sluts," bellows a guard,
"All of you will work here,
the rest of the day, clearing snow
and tending the fire till night.
Then you'll spread your legs
first for us guards, then for these ziks.
Then," he gives a manic laugh,
"If they will have you, for the dogs."

"No, for the love of God,"
the tall one cries,
"I am with child;
I will give birth next month."

"Your month is up," roars Pavlov,
and kicks her in the belly.
She falls, gasping, crawling.

Axes flash. Pavlov lies
in six pieces in the snow.

Rifles snap to the ready,
dogs strain at the leash,
no one breathes.

Then the escort troops
are pushing the women back aboard,
the door slams shut,
the engine lurches, the train moves on,
northward, for the Arctic camps;
and in silence we resume our work.

Chen Tsao-Fen

There is a story about two men crossing a frozen river. One is fearful of every step, but the other tries the ice with his staff, and then walks boldly across.

I belonged to a discussion group, and we began a protest against the professors at the local university, who refused to include any western sources in their teaching. Then we moved on to protest about other matters, and so became involved in the nationwide democracy movement. I was in charge of logistics, making sure there were transport, food, and medical supplies for the protesters. I never attended any demonstrations myself, and I always urged that there must be no violence.

The leader of the group made notes of our strategy meetings, and had written comments beside my recommendations, such as "Very good, Chen," and so on. This was what got me arrested after Tiananmen. They told me I would be in jail three years. I asked, "Can I have books?" They said "Yes." I thought, *Then that is not too bad, I will treat this period as my graduate study*. But in fact prisoners were not allowed books. I was able to obtain them only because my parents had influence.

As a political prisoner, I was not beaten like the other convicts. I was in a dormitory with twenty common criminals. Without this experience, I would never have learned about the dirty and desperate side of Chinese society. Some of the men were illiterate, and I taught them how to read.

After six months, I was put on trial. I was never allowed to meet with my lawyer, or my family, or anyone else. We had stopped a troop train that was going to Beijing at the time of Tiananmen and they found an obscure law against disrupting transportation. So I was sentenced to a year, which meant I was freed six months later. My fellow prisoners were sorry when I was released. They said, "If we had not been in prison with you, we would never have learned how to read."

Isaac Babel
Born 1894, executed 1940

Spectacles on your nose and autumn in your heart,
gripping an empty automatic,
you rode with an army of Cossacks.
You missed nothing: a dead horse on a Polish grave,
a blackening sabre wound, the rain-filled wind,
the murmur of dying Jews, the smell of smoke.
You never could forget that stifling scream
you choked on in a pogrom long ago.

Master of silence, from such you carved
a crown of thorns.
Times changed, and when you died
(a bullet like a period exactly placed),
did you find yourself sleeping among the stubble,
your horse tethered to your foot again,
the damp and groaning darkness streaming across
the plain, stars blowing through your hair?

Hideki Yukawa
Nobel laureate in Physics, 1949

How peaceful it is not to be noticed!
My schoolfriends called me Gonbei,
Hall of Quiet Thoughts.
Once, when I was in the first grade,
a girl gave me a handful of cherry blossoms.

The distance and mass
of the particle are inversely related.
I postulated the existence of the meson,
and calculated its mass
as 200 times that of the electron.

When we lived in the house with the stone lanterns
at Higashizakura, my brothers and I used to play
in the graveyard of the Jóken Temple.
I slipped and struck my head against a grave marker.
For a moment I saw darkness, and then sunbeams
through the leaves of the cherry trees.
Years later, with the idea of the meson,
I caught a memory of those midday stars.

Her ear lobes were just like the petals
of the cherry blossoms that she gave me.

Marie Curie at the Front

Since before dawn I've driven from aid post
to hospital to casualty clearing station,
demonstrating, observing, correcting the surgeons
as they use X-rays for the first time.
These wounded boys, dying many of them,
but smiling to see me.
If only Pierre were with me! Alas!
Alas.

I wept when I left Poland,
little more than a girl when I came to Paris.
I cooked in my attic, carried coal up six flights,
studying night and day
to catch up with the lycée graduates.
I was lost in the great city
and supremely happy.

And then I met Pierre.
I shall never forget him,
his hair haloed by the big window,
tall, grave, and gentle,
already respected by older scientists.
We were married. We bought two bicycles
to ride into the country;
that was our honeymoon.

We had an old shed provided by the School of Physics.
There we worked on concentrating radium,
freezing in winter, suffocating in summer,
broken by fatigue at the day's end,
and after the first years, never feeling really well.
In the evening, the bottles glowed softly in the dusk.
There we passed the best and happiest years of our life.
We worked in the preoccupation of a dream.
We were blessed with two daughters and a Nobel prize.

The other day I went back to see
the shed in which we worked,
before they pulled it down.
His writing was on the blackboard still,
his spirit permeated the place,
I waited for him to walk through the door.

The wagon wheel crushed his skull
and killed him instantly.

In his study, after the funeral,
the water buttercups
we had brought from the country
were still fresh.

Nocturne

There is always a source of light
in the paintings of Jakub Schikaneder,
and so it is in this one,
Nocturne, Old Prague, 1911.

In a dignified quarter of the city,
the glow of a gaslight
is diffused by the mist of the autumn dusk,
an autumn of damp pavements, wood smoke,
dead leaves, and early nightfall.

Above the bare trees, a window is open,
the room within lit warm by firelight
and in the window
the painter has placed a touch of red
where someone waits in the twilight;

a figure by the window, watching and waiting,
at the end of the long Hapsburg evening,
before the beginning of the night.

The Dead Child by Jakub Schikaneder

The candle on the chair beside the bed still glows,
and in the yellow light its last inch throws,
you can see the lips are cheerful, eager still,
as if she has not yet quite had her fill
of the bedtime story you were reading her.
And from her shoulders on the pillow you might infer
that before the story's end, she fell asleep.
Tread softly by her bed, don't talk or weep;
say, if you will, a final, silent prayer,
and brush and part for one last time the golden hair
above the unlined brow, and gently close
her hands together, and in them place a rose.

Edvard Munch: The Sick Child

I painted the sick child propped against pillows
just as I remembered my sister Sophie.
Her head is turned toward her mother
whose shoulders are bowed and face hidden.
I painted the sorrow of the child
for herself, and for her mother's grief.

In this painting I broke new ground. For which
my fellow-painters abused me in the street.

For weeks I labored on the hand,
resting weakly on the counterpane.
A hand is as interesting as a face,
but you do not paint a hand,
only how someone felt about that hand.
I painted a cold, pale, exhausted, empty hand.

The breakthrough was in my heart.

The Sculptor of Conques

Heaven is the same everywhere.
Go look at Moissac, at Vezelay,
all those predictable angels, saints, apostles.
So I carved heaven first.
Gave pride of place of course to Arosnide,
our first abbot, whose holy theft
brought us the relics of St. Foy.
But hell is where the payoff is.
Whom you condemn, roasts for eternity.
They're all here: the sinners,
the enemies of the Abbey,
and the enemies of mine.
Pride, sloth, avarice, slander,
forgery, covetousness, heresy, and fraud.
Demons with clubs driving miscreants
into the mouths of monsters.
And then the flames, the noose, the pincers,
the boiling cauldron, the toad at the feet,
the snake entering the socket of the eye.
I've shown Abbott Bégon, who stole the abbey silver,
groveling naked at the feet of a demon.
And Marevoy that persistent poacher
on the abbey lands, who also cheated me at cards,
tied over the flames on a spit turned by a rabbit.
At the bottom of the tympanum, I've placed the text,
Penis iniusti cruciatur,
the wicked are tormented by their punishments
in ignibus usti demonas,
in flames among the devils
tremunt perpetuoque gemunt,
they tremble and groan forever.

And now the last touches to this couple,
Bergova of the big breasts,
who spurned my offer of holy matrimony,
and went and fornicated with Jens the miller.
What is the punishment for lust?
I've shown them not in torment,
but in anticipation, standing naked before Satan,
into whose ear a devil whispers;
and you know that what he is proposing
is the worst thing you can imagine
and other things even worse than that.
I tell you, it pleased me to the marrow,
this hell of mine, that will last a thousand years.

The Builders of the Parthenon

Obedient to the dream of Pericles,
inspired by our master Phidias,
we planned, designed, and built,
brought sculptors in from Attica and Thebes
to carve the centaurs, warriors,
bodies entangled in ecstasy or war,
gigantic figures on the giant frieze;
the whole, not static but alive,
Pythagoras' geometry in stone,
elegance of an argument by Socrates.
To what effect? Athens, diminished, like a ghost,
the temple, in one century a mosque,
in others full of monks upon their knees,
broken stones under the crucifix,
the lion, the crescent, Swastika,
all crowded now with Germans, Japanese;
who now remembers us,
the builders of the Parthenon,
Iktinus and Kalikrates?

Daylight Saving

All his life he loved the daylight. As a young man, he worked in a factory for five years until he had saved enough to buy a farm. He rose before dawn to milk the cows, then spent the day outdoors. He discovered a way to save daylight, using a series of focused parabolic mirrors to funnel the light into an old zinc beer keg.

Now he was old, and spent much of his time indoors. He rolled his wheelchair to the tool chest, and found an adjustable wrench. Laboriously, he maneuvered his way into the yard. He fitted the wrench to the valve on the keg and gave it a quarter-turn. It emitted a sharp hiss. He readjusted the wrench, took a deep breath, and turned the valve wide open. The keg exploded in a blinding flash, and he rode into eternity on a beam of brilliant light.

Uncle Jake

His brothers all did medicine or law,
but he took on the farm and made it pay.
Although the land was rocky and the soil was poor,
he raised a herd of beef and crops of corn and hay.

But beavers built their dams across the creek,
flooded the fields, cut birch trees by the score,
and Uncle Jake, though usually meek,
blew up their dams and lodges: this was total war!

I saw him in the hospital, a week
before he died, when he was eighty-four;
shrunken and pallid, he could hardly speak.
I told him of the new lodge by the shore,
he grasped my wrist, sat up, his eyes grew bright:
Get dynamite, he roared, Get dynamite!

Exemptions

Had a run-in with Emma last week at the band office, Louie says. You know Emma. Two hundred and fifty pounds, beat up her husband in the pool hall last month. She wanted us to hold out for a better price from the printers, and when I got off the phone after I'd closed the deal, she said, "You're always trying to do a favor for the white man, aren't you? You fair-skinned people are all the same, you want to be like white men." I'd had enough. I said, "Listen to me, I've lived every day of my life, 47 years, on the Res. When I was in school I was too light to be an Indian and too dark to be a white kid. My skin hasn't exempted me from anything. It hasn't exempted me from growing up in one room with eleven brothers and sisters. It hasn't exempted me from seeing my father passed out every other evening. It hasn't exempted me from sitting in the car for six hours on a freezing night waiting for my parents to come out of the hotel. It hasn't exempted me from seeing my uncles and aunts beating the piss out of one another. It hasn't exempted me from any of the shit of being an Indian in this country." Then I went in my office and shut the door. Well, ten minutes later there's a knock on the door, and she comes in, tears streaming down her face. "I guess I owe you an apology," she says.

At Street Corners

It was on some Greek island, Rhodes, I think,
just after your 50th birthday,
though no one, especially a Greek,
would think you over 35.

An elderly man with white mustache,
looked up as you walked by
and instinctively raised his panama,
and you were happy all day.

Thus would I transmogrify myself
into a series of distinguished gentlemen
—widowers with married daughters,
who played chess at the taverna in the evenings—
and appear in different guises, at street corners
on days when you were sad
to raise my hat to you.

Odysseus and the Siren

What Homer says is that Odysseus
was serenaded by the Sirens with these words:
"We know the pains that Greeks and Trojans
once endured upon the spreading plain of Troy,"
and so, we may infer, he realized
that they could understand him in a way
that those who'd stayed at home could not.

What Homer didn't say was that the claim
to understand is equally a plea for empathy,
and being one who never missed a cry for help,
Odysseus broke the leather thongs
that tied him to the mast,
escaped the grabbing hands,
dived overboard, swam to the rock
where a Siren, her blonde hair falling
on her breasts, sat singing her angelic songs.
She reached for him as he climbed through the surf
and then was gone, to grace a distant rock
her pleading song more heavenly still.

Surprised, he dived again,
knowing that all the battles fought,
the escapes and journeyings
had been a preparation for this day.
Then, like a mirage, she had moved once more.
Doggedly, again he gathered strength,
and plunged into the desolate waves.
But as he clambered up the black volcanic rock,
bleeding from torn feet and hands,
her voice and blue beseeching eyes
calling him still, he was once more alone.

At which he stood a moment, salt water
streaming from his beard and reddened eyes,
then, like a great bear, he shook his head,
dived back into the treacherous foam,
and struck out for his ship.
He took the rudder, signaled to his men,
and set the course for Ithaca and home.

I Am the King, Your Father

The boy walked with intent, well-made and tall.
at his heels a hound and in his hand a spear.
I stepped out from the shadow of the wall;
"Who are you?" he asked. "What brings you here?"
I saw myself, then, as he saw me,
grizzled beard, clothes roughly patched with hide,
burned and bowed with muscle from the years at sea.
"I am the King, your father," I replied.
"The King? My father? Odysseus?" he said.
I answered: "I am the father whom you never knew.
A father who forfeited his son." I bowed my head.
He said, "I have waited all my life for you."
So ended the long vigil we both had kept;
we fell into each other's arms, and wept.

Sweet Wells

How can I explain you? To feel what is Greece, it is completely silence. To understand, you have—I am missing the word—you have to be passioned. Sometimes we go to church in Holy Week just in order to cry. Because of the songs! Because of the smells! The sad is for a moment. Then the laughter comes and takes the sad away. To be in the moment of complete satisfaction, mind, body, and soul, for the ancient Greeks was the time to die.

I feel you in my skin, you are in my hair, you are in my eyes. Yes, the saints and the ancient gods, but things are not so simple to answer like that, it is too much different, a long talk, it takes years. We have icons to keep the saints, our beloveds, close to us. Some people also keep snakes in their houses. To keep the happiness in the house. To keep the rats down? Ela, bullshit, don't be so Nordic. That is your western rationality. That is the wisdom of Athena. I am speaking of the wisdom of Apollo, the power of light, of being yourself, of being free and beautiful and having the god inside.

I don't want to complicate you anymore. Don't try to analyze all this out, you will get crazy. You come from a different country, there is a bigger difference, bigger than the Gorge of Samaria. I feel you in my head, and in my heart, and in my breasts, and in my mouni. I could die at this moment because I am so happy. Let us sleep now.

In Nopigia

She cooks an omelet with oregano,
walking the kitchen tiles in tanned bare feet,
her sun-bleached hair in morning disarray.

Clothes dry outside, and on the village street
dogs bark in counterpoint and children play,
behind us on the hillside roosters crow.

In the still air, I hear a donkey bray.
I have a sense that something is complete,
though what it is exactly I don't know.

Her T-shirt shows a tree branch in the snow,
on it a snowy owl. Our final day
on the chapel-speckled mountainside of Crete.

Evangelos

There are three sorts of men.
Those who eat eggs without shells;
those who eat eggs and their shells;
and those who eat eggs, eggshells, and the eggcups.
The last are Cretan.

You have been married two years,
my father Evangelos would say,
When are you going to give me a grandson?
Then war came.
My father and my husband both
joined those in the mountains.
I went to the monastery and rolled cartridges
from ancient manuscripts
and pages torn from holy books.

The war ended and the men came back
with their wounds.
Our first child, a boy, was born.

My father would come to the door
of our house and roar,
Let me smell the caca! I want to smell the caca!
We named our son Evangelos.

On a Cuban Street

The many-coloured women of Santiago
are proud and elegant as antelope.
Their scent mingles with mimosa,
salt spray from the seafront,
and the sweat of bicitaxi drivers.
A man offers me two live doves in a paper bag;
a pig is trussed and squealing
on the back of a bicycle.
I stop to get the dust cleaned from my shoes
by an old man shriveled and bent;
I imagine he sleeps in a shed
at the back of somebody's house.
His skin is as black as his polish,
which he deftly applies with his fingers
then buffs with a rag full of holes
until the leather reflects
his ancient yellow eyes.
The usual price is ten cents,
but I have no change.
I hand him a three peso note;
he gives a cry like a wounded bird.

Plaza Vieja, Havana

More and more often these days, we see him put his book down beside his coffee cup, or sometimes not open it, and gaze across the square as if he expected to see her come toward him, just as she did thirty years ago.

The winter sunshine falls on baroque balconies, the fountain sparkles, a three-legged dog hops across the cobble stones, a gaggle of school girls break into spontaneous dance, voices rise among the players of dominoes. Would he recognize her now? Is she still alive? And if so, in which country does she live?

Did he, in fact, see her, at that last moment? Was that why, when he slumped forward in his seat, the waiter, who hurried toward him, saw the beginning of a smile on his lips, and a light slowly fading in his eyes?

Hotel du Cygne

Last sunlight on the golden stone of the city
and on the new chestnut leaves as green
as the lizard I saw in Provence.
Dazed from the highway I walk
round the old quarter. In a narrow street
a name catches my eye: Hotel du Cygne.
And there it is. Blank cream-coloured front,
huge archway into the courtyard,
and the hanging cast-iron sign of a swan.
On the top floor the shutters
of one of the dormer windows are open,
and that must have been our room.
I remember the dark beams and the sloping ceiling
and climbing the steep stairs late in the evenings
at the end of the summer years ago
at the end of our life together.

In the Uffizi

Deep Rafael eyes
head chiseled by Michelangelo
a curl of dark hair below the ear
Botticelli sweep of nose and chin
Madonna, la custoda,
in black slacks and blue shirt
leans against a doorway
checking the tickets of tourists
blinded by the old paintings
on the walls.

King David's Spring

White sandstone canyon walls
like the layers of a dream
as I walk
into the furnace of En-Gedi.
With harsh cries black birds
launch themselves from the cliffs;
two fighters split the sky.
Dust puffs at my feet
and I think of the ashes
of a million children.

A patch of greenery below
in the arid valley. Palm trees
like the few righteous gentiles.

I climb down the cliff,
walk up the wadi, and from far off
I hear the deep note of falling water.
The path turns, and before me
fed by a waterfall
is a long pool as green as the psalms.

I drop my pack and wade into the water,
deep, Abba, father,
deep enough to swim in,
down to the cascade and stand up
stand up
and let the waters of Israel thunder on my head.

The Potter's Husband

He was a quiet man,
the man whose house I rented
in New Zealand.
I came across a few poems he had written.
His wife had been a potter;
she'd died five years before.

I burned trash
in the incinerator in the yard
Once, when it wouldn't light,
I threw in a cup of gasoline.
When I picked myself up
my skin smelled like a forest fire.

In rain storms
the steel roof sounded like
ten thousand tin drums.
The flesh of papayas
was the colour of sunsets.
One morning the kids said,
You were gasping for breath last night.
I said, Yes,
I dreamed I was being smothered
by koala bears.

All over the house I kept finding
small pieces of broken pottery.

The Poems of Judith Pond

The wound in the palm of the hand.
The hand in the wound in the side.
Sunlight in darkness.
The dark at the center of the sun.
The voice at the end of the dark.
The poems of Judith Pond.

Hair black as the pupils of eyes
dilated in the dusk.
A dove captured and fluttering. A dove
grey softer than dawn and dying.
An hourglass. A skull. The green intelligence
of late spring.
A nun, chosen and unaware,
under a fig tree dreaming of a troubadour.
Olive oil poured on stones warmed by the sun,
olive oil poured on the pale skin
of shoulders made thinner by winter
and by summer.
The midnight arrival without passport or maps.
A period between two spaces.
From the void, energy;
from energy, fire;
from fire, light:
the poems of Judith Pond.

The Abersychan Writers Group

Dai? says Gwen.
"No," says Dai,
"I've not brought anything today.
But I can recite the whole of Gunga Din.
From memory. Tell me when to stop—"
"Stop!" everybody yells.

Abersychan: along the green valley
houses march shoulder to shoulder.
The empty mines now stand like monuments,
and from brick chapels I seem to hear
the echo of miners singing hymns
on their pittance of Sunday sunshine.

"Well, Iestyn, will you read?" says Gwen.

Put two Welshmen together, it's said,
and you have a choir. Take one away
and you have a poet.

"Hello my darlings! Hello my angels!"
Ifor comes in, his bus was late.
"I won't say she's easy," Dai says to Huw,
"but she's the only girl I know
who has a ripcord in her knickers."

"Now you're winding me up," Gwen says.
"Can we get started? Iestyn?"

Iestyn, sixteen, brown hair
streaked with blond,
hesitates, then reads his poem:
wrath and rain, his mother's
wombing and wishwork.

"Ah, there's beautiful," says Dai.

Kari Leaves Home

My swing hangs from the apple tree.
Boughs are bent with fruit,
wasps buzz among fallen plums.
The rose hips are as big as cherries.

How will I live without the music
of the wind on the fjord?
Of the waterfall?
Of the tumbling river,
its colours changing with the light?
Every morning of my life I have wakened
to the sound of sheep bells.

My father said,
you can go to Oslo and become a doctor,
or you can stay here and marry Ragnar
and clean fish the rest of your life.

Little farms at the mountain foot,
their green fields sloping to the water.
Sod-roofed houses of red board;
the graves of my grandparents
outside my father's tiny church.

Ragnar will not take his boat out today.
He does not want to see the ferry pass.

How will people know me
who do not know
the place from which I come?

Leaving Palm Springs

Smooth sensual skin
of the eucalyptus outside my window;
in the mauve blossom
of the jacaranda, hummingbirds
whirr like small electric motors.

The wind rattles the palms at night
with the suck and flap of the sea;
as I tread
the bright early morning sidewalk
I crunch olives underfoot.

A green caesura
in the parching desert
where poets in their BMWs
are calmed by the waters under the earth.

The wind on the highway punishes my car.
Like the arms of synchronized swimmers,
the blades of windmills
wave me goodbye.

On Wolfe Island

Listening to your voice I understand
why strangers ask you in bars
to speak at their funerals.

We sit at the table behind your cottage
in the sunshine,
which you call the laughter of God.
We watch the ducklings swimming
in the shallow water
and talk of the woman we both love.

And you say, to be a writer
only two things are necessary:
you have to be hungry,
and you have to be free.

After an Absence

We learn to countenance our parents' age with grace;
the glasses and the cane are not undignified.
Tell me, what solace can philosophy provide
when I observe a new line in my daughter's face?

Part of a Biography of a Garden

I see a garden gone to seed,
grass long and untended,
poppies and hollyhocks blazing insistently
through flowerbeds of weeds,
apples glowing against a wall.

I see a young man pushing a mower
while a young woman prunes roses.
Against the fence, a row of tomatoes;
the apple tree is bearing again,
and a bird bath stands on the lawn.

I see the young man in uniform,
standing stiffly with his wife.
The lawn is still carefully mown,
roses are blooming,
the bird bath is empty.

I see a woman with child,
her hand to her mouth,
in her other hand a telegram,
unaware of the garden
with its neat rows of vegetables.

I see a black rabbit in a wire run,
beside it a girl in school uniform,
standing next to her mother
shy and straight among dandelions
against a wall rich with apples.

I see a young woman sitting
outdoors drinking tea with her mother
on a lawn that is smooth and green,
and beyond them poppies and roses,
and apples coming ripe in the sun.

Prairie Graveyard

Two almost strangers
from the long highway almost friends
leaving the broken-down motel
to walk the avenues of graves
outside the town
as the red sun sets,
and night impends.

Epitaphs of survivors
of dust storms, blizzards, smallpox,
drought, war, the death of children,
the contempt of politicians.

A flash of gold and grey: a fox
stops on the path, looks back, and trots away.

Marble. Stone. Fresh flowers on an ancient grave.
Names, dates, a verse, a prayer.
A wooden board carved only with a name.
Early moonlight. This moment. Your black erotic hair.

Voyageur
In Memory of Bill Peruniak, 1932-2004

When the wind is from the west,
he says, the ice is like a battering ram.
Last spring, a sheet a metre thick,
embedded with a one-ton rock,
was pushed up vertically,
almost to the height of where we stand.
You can see how the shoreline
has eroded and collapsed.

It's Christmas. But no snow yet.
We stir coffee, share memories,
look out across the water from the deck.
I'm taking the big canoes up north
this summer. One more time.

Let me show you what I've done.
The water was low and winter late this year.
I poured a two-foot concrete pad,
collected rocks from all along the lake.

Yes, it has metastasized.
Too late for chemo or for surgery.

We climb down the ladder
to the stony beach. For me, he says,
this is like writing my will.

Set in black mortar, his testament
is a six-foot wall of limestone blocks,
confronting the water
like a voyageur, head on,
foursquare against the winter storms
and the pounding ice of spring.

Missionaries

Coastal Nigeria, the White Man's Grave:
where the rain brought floods,
the droughts starvation;
they worked there twenty years,
this missionary couple, sustained
through plague, smallpox, malaria
by their devotion to Jesus and each other.

Africa entered their bones;
they made converts, built a church,
founded a school, a hospital, traveled
on bicycles they'd brought from Britain,
shiny at first, soon rusty and ramshackle,
but most impressive to the local men,
whose one ambition was, one day, to own a bike.

Broken in health,
they were posted to the drier north
to work in their advancing years
among the turbaned Moslem tribes.
Facing retirement, in their seventies,
they made a sentimental journey south
to see again the district of their prime.

They found their old church active still,
though disaffiliated,
only a bit decayed, and painted on the wall
its name and dedication:
Church of Jesus Christ, Bicyclist.

Sheep Market

The oak trees along the river
are changing from gold to green,
an old man throws bread to the ducks
as I cross the bridge to the market
where the pens are crowded with lambs;
Suffolk, black-face, and white-face,
speckle-face, Hampshires, and crosses.

They trot down the ramps
from small mud-spattered trailers.
Gates open in front of them,
close behind them. They move
from pen to pen at a whistle
or the wave of an arm or a crook.
Two days without water or food,
they jostle and bleat and cough
and, where there is room,
scratch with an awkward hoof;
but mostly they stand and wait.

These are early spring lambs
for the ovens of England,
bred out of season,
born at Christmas
on the green hills of Wales.

An inspector presses backs
to check fatness,
then sticks a label
on the rail of a pen,
which a lamb promptly eats.

The auctioneer rings his bell,
then moves with the buyers
down the long line of pens
while the farmers, their jackets
and raincoats and caps
brown and green as spring earth,
lean on their sticks
talking subsidies, prices, and weights.

When the last pen is sold,
the big trucks back up to the gates.
A driver, cigarette in mouth,
opens great doors, moves a barrier,
and the lambs, released from the pen,
dash up the ramp
into the truck's dark interior.

But one lamb jumps the barrier,
and sturdy and fast as a young bull,
takes off across the market, veering
and reversing as two perspiring men,
shouting and laughing, run to intercept it.
They corner it beside the auction shed;
the great doors of the truck
close behind it. I hear
the sound of bleating from within
and I see barbed wire, dogs,
watch towers, and searchlights,
as I move off down the street
to the shops, to look for mint sauce,
and Mozart's Requiem.

I Am Cooking Jambalaya

with fresh shrimp, curry, raisins, onions,
parsley, basil, paprika, and thyme.
Asleep in the darkened bedroom,
you are under the quilt, out of sight.

Today we walked a long way
on the empty white beach.

When I brought you an orange this morning,
you said you'd hardly slept all night,
and when you did, you'd dreamed
that you were drawing symbols on the ground,
and at every point a plant grew up.
I didn't ask how you would have slept
if we'd made love. But
what greater sleeplessness
might then befall?

I am cooking jambalaya.
In a light spring rain
the dogwood trees are turning green.
Gusts of wind throb through the pines,
and blow last year's dead leaves along the ground.

Finishing Touches

In his old age he would reflect, as old men do, on a woman he once loved, and the table he built for her.

He drafted a design in Tudor style, found red oak, winter-cut and air dried. The top he made from six long boards, tongue and grooved. He turned the massive legs himself, watching with joy the curlicues of wood spin from the chisel tip.

He planed the pieces to an even thickness, then rough-sanded them with 60 and 120 grit. He used no metal anywhere. All the joints were mortice and tenon, drawbored with wooden pegs, enormously strong.

Once the table was solidly assembled, it stood blond, naked, smooth to the touch.

Now began the long task of finishing by hand. He used the best aluminum oxide paper, soaking the wood between each sanding to raise the grain. He was working with 220 grit the day she left.

Head down and shoulders bent, he labored on, inhaling the fine oak-scented dust, discarding the sanding block in order to sense irregularities with his finger tips. Down through the grades, 500, 800, 1000, 3000, stroking, burnishing the wood.

And finally, a beeswax polish to give a mirror finish, with a depth that lit the wood with an inner glow. Still he did not stop, muscles aching, hour by hour, day after day, rubbing, buffing, caressing, trying to perfect a surface as smooth and golden as her skin.

Moments

Moments like harp notes
Like pearls on a string
Like camels in the sunset
Like geese on the wing.

Moment of intent
Moment of affirmation
Moment of consent
Moment of confirmation.

In the flash of the lightning
The drumming of the rain
Like a dove to the dovecote
An arrow. A flame.

The Gift that's Unexpected

"What about love?" she says
She looks at me across the shrimp and oysters
We meet like this, every few months, to talk theology
I bite on something hard, and hope it's not a broken tooth

She looks at me across the shrimp and oysters
It's March: the southern air is soft and warm
I bite on something hard, and hope it's not a broken tooth
Along the causeway, pelicans dive for fish

It's March: the southern air is soft and warm
Across the bay, the *Alabama* looms
Along the causeway, pelicans dive for fish
I tongue the object from my mouth

Across the bay, the *Alabama* looms
Because she's here, the day is radiant
I tongue the object from my mouth
"The word made flesh," she says

Because she's here, the day is radiant
Between my fingers is a tiny pearl
"The word made flesh," she says
The gift that's unexpected is the best

Between my fingers is a tiny pearl
We meet like this, every few months, to talk theology
The gift that's unexpected is the best
"What about love?" she says.

Vanishing Point

Like perspective in a da Vinci drawing
the railway lines recede
through the sagebrush and cactus
of the Texas desert. At the horizon,
somewhere north of the last sunlight,
the tracks appear to meet;
but if you walk down them, you find
they just run parallel forever,
like your life and mine.

A distant whistle as I walk away.
I find three pennies in my pocket
and lay them on the rail. You really need
chewed gum to stick them down.
After the freight cars rumble by,
I find one, lying beside the track,
stretched, crushed, and burnished,
very thin, very smooth, very bright,
bearing only the ghost of its original design.

What I meant to say, though,
before the interruption of the train,
standing here in the righteous, celibate desert,
was about the railway tracks.
Do they run separately forever?
Or at night, in intervals of silence,
when the breeze smells of cactus blossom
and the sky is jewelry against black skin,
do they leave their places and entwine?

Doubt

Today I saw a statue
by Andrea del Verrocchio
of Christ and Doubting Thomas.
For an instant, I stopped breathing.
Christ raises a hand to expose
his wounded side, which Thomas
addresses tentatively with his fingertips.
But the feet—the feet of the disciple!
One points toward his Lord, and one away.
That was exactly how she stood
the morning I said I wanted to marry her,
one foot toward me, one seeking to escape.

Lazarus

Nothing, at first. And then the shout,
penetrating nothingness.
Lazarus!
Come out!

It echoes through the cave. I rise
still clothed in my own winding sheet;
I stagger with the cloth around my feet,
blindfolded by the linen round my eyes.

I hear astonished voices. I do not understand
that I'm alive. I smell the wind. I feel the sun.
The bandages fall off, undone
by a familiar woman's hand.

I know these folk. I recognize this place.
And there he is: we stumble to embrace.
With joy and awe I see the trace
of tears that streak his fierce and gentle face.

Old Miner

In memory of Jack Norman, 1886-1963

"I went to work at twelve
and at thirteen went down the pit.
In winter in those days
we saw the sun one day in seven.

"At five o'clock I walked
three miles to work and then
crawled two miles underground.
They paid us when we started at the face.
The galleries were two feet high;
you lay upon your side to use your pick."

That's how I see him, making his way
like Theseus through labyrinths of coal;
driving before him hate and fear,
gas, dust, and darkness, like the Minotaur.

A Good Death

A scrambling in the wood stove;
another sparrow
has come down the chimney.
I let her out;
she flies straight at the window,
hits the glass, drops dead:
free
and heading for the light.

Poodle

There was a big old groundhog, my brother said,
living under a wood pile in the field.
The dogs cornered him one time, all six of them.
He lay back and slashed and bit
and in the end they all backed off.
One dog lost the best part of an ear.
The poodle wanted to join in,
but just ran round the outside of the circle barking.
That poodle, I said, must have been a poet.

Potiphar's Wife

She lied, of course. So did he.
For months he had observed her dancer's feet,
how tenderly she used her slaves, her eyes
on him like green furnaces.
He turned his head, but in the end
he had foreseen everything in a dream.

And she—she'd watched this foreigner
with his sunburned face,
strange speech, and alien god;
his fingers deft on the lyre, loyal to her husband,
the Chief of Police, a generous but boring man.

That was before the day she saw him
through the reeds, this Hebrew,
diving naked into the river.
Now the memory inflamed her
every time she put into her mouth a ripe plum
thrown down by a tame monkey
in her lush Nilotic orchard.

She found him asleep
in the empty house. She knew the penalty:
for him, a thousand stripes;
for her, amputation of the nose.
His eyes opened. She loosed
the golden buckle at her waist.

The Canopic Jars

"Look how exquisitely each lid
is fashioned in the likeness of a son of Horus.
Imnesty, with the human head
will hold my liver,
ape-headed Hapi will preserve my lungs."

"What of the brain?" I asked.
"The brain," she said, "is unimportant,
and is discarded before embalming. See,
the stomach goes in this one,
under the jackal-headed Diamintef."

"And the heart?" I stole a glance at her.
"Yes, the heart, the center of intelligence,
we leave inside the body when it's mummified.
This last jar, for my intestines,
is Quebehsennef with the falcon's head."
Her fingers on the lid were sensitive and deft.

But her face! Her rapt face. Desolate.
Bereft.

Tango Lesson

"Give me belly," she says. "Back straight.
Knees bent. In the tango, you lead from here:
she strokes my chest. Your right hand
is too tentative, as if my back is bare,
but it's a good cotton shirt I have on.
Five, six, seven, eight. Now open me.
Hand lower, no, not that low."

She steps back and gives herself a shake.
She says: "I must tell you about the tango.
The goucho comes in from the wind,
into the warm and candlelit cantina.
He steps between the crowded tables
with their bottles of wine,
under the low, smoke-blackened beams.
He paces with a stalking motion,
like el puma, the big black panther.
The woman of the cantina dances with him,
joined together at the hips.
but their shoulders apart disdainfully,
She implores him to stay, and he consents—
for one more dance.

"The tango is like passion,
that burns out with its own satiation.
It is like love, which does not endure.
It is like life, that inexorably
goes forward to its end.

"Now hold me like you mean it."

Sebastian

As a child, his parents took him to the Staatliche in Berlin. There he saw Botticelli's San Sebastian, pierced with many arrows. That night he woke up screaming.

But that was years ago, before he joined and then became a section leader in the Hitler Youth. It was on his eighteenth birthday that he leapt from the open door of the Junker 52, a hundred metres above the sunburned soil of Crete.

He kept tight hold on his weapon, flexed his knees, prepared to roll, watched out for rocks below. But there was only greenery in view.

Alas and woe, for the boy who fell among bamboo.

Yes, We Had Comrades

Sixty of us jumped, late one December day,
into Dien Bien Phu, the last contingent, their last hope.
Dropping through searchlights and artillery fire,
chutes shot to ribbons, men died without a chance to fight,
in thirty minutes eight legionnaires were dead.
We others reached the fort to cries of "Vive la France!"

Six of the legionnaires who fought for France
were Germans, and they'd formed a choir, that was the day
I heard the Choirboys first. Both baritones were dead,
but tenor and bass voices rang with pride and hope.
Heads shaved, tattooed, they sang of how we'd fight
till we were overrun or perished under fire.

Our strongpoint had one howitzer; the Viet Minh returned our fire
with ten. Every plane bringing mail from France,
or fresh supplies, was shot out of the air. We'd fight
them back, lay down new wire and mines each day,
each night their lines moved closer. Now our only hope
was honor and remembrance after we were dead.

In January, fighting hand-to-hand, our post was overrun. The dead
were left unburied. On the forced march guards would fire
at wounded stragglers. We trudged on in the hope
of an armistice between Saigon and France.
In prison camp we grieved and starved by day,
by night men shouted in their sleep as they relived the fight.

The Germans decided this was not their fight;
got double rations with the slogan, Better Red than Dead,
and sang the *Internationale* at roll call every day.
One morning the Commandant reported that concentrated fire
at Dien Bien Phu had wiped out the last legionnaire from France.
"Well? Sing!" He ordered. We watched the choir with fear and hope.

And they began to sing. Men hung their heads. We lost all hope,
except for me and other hotheads, who jumped up to fight.
But then we recognized the song we'd sometimes heard in France:
Ich hatt einen Kamaraden, the haunting hymn in honour of their dead.
We cheered and wept and sang till guards began to fire
their weapons in the air. Our celebration went on all day.

The Choirboys' act that day restored our hope.
Their hymn put new fire in our hearts and helped us fight
to keep faith with the dead, till peace was signed, and we returned to France.

Apprehensions of Van Gogh

The old man shuffles across the room towards me, and I see he's not so old, forty, or thirty-five. "It's muddy outside," he says. "I like your boots. Do you like mine? You're getting old. Your hair is gray." He laughs. "I lost a tooth, see? You've had a good shave. I shaved today, here, feel my chin. Where are your kids? My kid died." He begins to cry.

This, Vincent, was your dread.

It's awkward to point a pistol at your chest. At the heart that ached for miners, beggars, prostitutes, potato eaters; and expanded for the sun and sunflowers, for ripe corn and the deep green of cypress trees.

The function of the ribs is to protect the heart, and one of them stopped the bullet.

Well, it gave time for your brother to come, sit by your bed, while you weakened from infection and loss of blood. Time to fill your pipe, talk a little, like old companions, for a night and a day. At the end you said "We've been good friends, Theo." Then you were quiet, until the pipe dropped from your hand.

Author Bio Note:

My parents were missionaries in China, and when Japanese bombers attacked the town where they were living in 1939, my mother returned to England, where I was born. My father remained in China for two more years, then decided he wanted a more active role in the war. He made his way back to England, where he took charge of a small country parish, and joined the Army Intelligence Corps. He had fought in the trenches in World War I and had been commissioned. In the Second War, he rose to the rank of major.

Some of my earliest recollections are of German bombers going over nightly on their way to London, and on the way back dropping their unused bombs on our village. In the morning we would examine the bomb craters and the remains of V-I rockets. The war was endlessly fascinating. This perhaps accounts for the interest in war evident in some of my poems, while my rural upbringing is reflected in the pastoral element in others. I composed my first poem, a limerick, when I was 7.

At nine, in line with the British custom of delegating parenthood, I was sent away to boarding school. I learned little there, but did get occasional encouragement to write. One teacher paid me the compliment of insisting that a story of mine was plagiarized, as the theme was too adult for my years. We were encouraged to memorize poetry, and to perform in Shakespeare plays. At thirteen I moved on to a good grammar school. I was far behind the other students, and was consistently bottom of my class. The years of mid-adolescence are a time when young people should be laying down a firm foundation in science, mathematics, modern languages, and the arts. I spent them learning Latin and Greek. However, in my last two years I had a brilliant English teacher, who introduced us to contemporary verse, and instilled in us, at least in me, a lifelong love of poetry and literature. I had at last learned how to play the academic game, and won two scholarships to Oxford.

In vacations I worked at various times as a highway construction laborer, letter carrier, detective's assistant, and forest fire crew. I also taught for several months in private and public schools before and after university. One summer I flew to Canada with a group of students, worked 66 hours a week in a factory for six weeks, then hitchhiked across Canada and into the US, bought a car for $50 and drove it back to the east coast where I sold it as scrap for $5.

In my first 21 years living in Europe, I visited the Continent only twice. I hitchhiked to a work camp in France, where I first learned to appreciate Romanesque art, and then went on to Barcelona, where I saw my first bull fight. I was specializing in the Italian Renaissance, which entailed learning Italian, and one spring I drove my motor bike to Rome, where I saw John XXIII give his Easter blessing in St. Peter's Square.

After leaving Oxford with a degree in Modern History, I spent a year as a special student at Harvard, studying psychology and theology. I then moved to Canada to teach at the secondary level. Like most teachers, I learned on the job, and each year was more satisfying than the last. It was my experience that school teachers treat one another with more civility and respect than do people in most other occupations. I taught History and English in Northern Ontario, directed plays, snow shoed to school through the bush, and experienced temperatures down to -48C. One winter day, I was out deer hunting with a colleague when he said, "You should go and take a Ph.D. You're wasting your time in the classroom." I don't think anyone wastes time teaching, but this was a new idea. I found a program in Educational Theory at the University of Toronto, which offered enough financial support to live at the poverty level. I completed the master's and doctoral program in a little over three years, and was offered a position at Queen's University. There I stayed for 28 years.

I had married, and my wife and I were blessed with three wonderful children, two daughters and a son, who from then on became my principal priority. But my work also absorbed me. My doctoral research had been on analysing prejudice in school text books, but this was too narrow a field to retain my interest. I taught curriculum planning, and found that the only text book worthy of the name was the Instructional Design Manual for the US Armed Forces. I resolved to fill this gap. I started writing while we were on sabbatical in Oxford, where I taught at the Institute of Education, and finished five years later. The 500 page book was quickly picked up by Harcourt Brace Jovanovich, whose editors were a joy to work with. The book was favourably received, and sold well in North America and elsewhere.

We had a house built for us in a suburb and settled down to an almost stereotyped middle class existence. I was publishing academic papers, and I produced a few more books. I was on the road and in the air a lot. I enjoyed teaching, particularly in graduate and technical programs where the students were mature and dedicated professionals. It has been well said that being a professor in a North American university is the best job in the Western world.

My marriage ended. I took another sabbatical and went with the children to New Zealand, where they survived the tough school system for two semesters. I was a guest at a New Zealand university, where I got considerable exposure to the Marxist theory of everything. We came back via Fiji, the Cook Islands, and Tahiti, places that have become dream-like in my recollection.

My children went to university and moved into professions, one as a teacher and two as social workers. I am happy to report that they are all better people than I am. For a long time I had nurtured the idea of becoming a full-time writer. I entered a short story in a local competition. It won the $500 prize and was published in the local paper. This modest success was seductive. The time came when I could afford to leave the university and live if not in luxury, at least in sufficiency. I turned down a lucrative offer to continue teaching and wrote a short story on my first day as a free-lance.

I soon learned that publishing was much harder in the literary world than in academe. I spent my first two years researching and writing a novel that remains unpublished to this day. But I learned tenacity, and within a few years I had published poems and short fiction in over 100 literary journals in Canada, the US, Britain, and Australia. I spent my summers in Canada and escaped the winters to Spain, France, Greece, Cuba, and the southern United States. I studied the languages in the countries I lived in, and at one time or another could converse in French, Spanish, Italian, Greek, and German. Altogether, I travelled to about 35 countries. Many of my poems and stories spring from the places I have visited and the people I have encountered.

Writing is one of least parasitic of occupations. It consumes very little by way of communal resources, and it creates something which did not previously exist. I hope to continue writing until I draw my last breath.

Books in the North Shore Series
Find full information at
– http://www.HiddenBrookPress.com/b-NShore.html

2 Anthologies

Changing Ways is a book of prose by Cobourg area authors including: Jean Edgar Benitz, Patricia Calder, Fran O'Hara Campbell, Leonard D'Agostino, Shane Joseph, Brian Mullally. Editor: Jacob Hogeterp
– Prose – ISBN – 978-1-897475-22-5

That Not Forgotten – Editor – Bruce Kauffman with 118 authors from the North Shore geographic area.
– Prose and Poetry – ISBN – 978-1-897475-89-8

First set of five books

— M.E. Csamer – Kingston – *A Month Without Snow*
– Prose – ISBN – 978-1-897475-87-2
— Elizabeth Greene – Kingston – *The Iron Shoes*
– Poetry – ISBN – 978-1-897475-76-6
— Richard Grove – Brighton – *A Family Reunion*
– Prose – ISBN – 978-1-897475-90-2
— R.D. Roy – Trenton – *A Pre emptive Kindness*
– Prose – ISBN – 978-1-897475-80-3
— Eric Winter – Cobourg – *The Man In The Hat*
– Poetry – ISBN – 978-1-897475-77-3

Second set of five books

— Janet Richards – Belleville – *Glass Skin*
– Poetry – ISBN – 978-1-897475-01-0
— R.D. Roy – Trenton – *Three Cities*
– Poetry – ISBN – 978-1-897475-96-4
— Wayne Schlepp – Cobourg – *The Darker Edges of the Sky*
– Poetry – ISBN – 978-1-897475-99-5
— Benjamin Sheedy – Kingston – *A Centre in Which They Breed*
– Poetry – ISBN – 978-1-897475-98-8
— Patricia Stone – Peterborough – *All Things Considered*
– Prose – ISBN – 978-1-897475-04-1

Third set of five books

— Mark Clement – Cobourg – *Island In the Shadow*
  – Poetry – ISBN – 978-1-897475-08-9
— Anthony Donnelly – Brighton – *Fishbowl Fridays*
  – Prose – ISBN – 978-1-897475-02-7
— Chris Faiers – Marmora – *ZenRiver Poems & Haibun*
  – Poetry – ISBN – 978-1-897475-25-6
— Shane Joseph – Cobourg – *Fringe Dwellers* Second Edition
  – Prose – ISBN – 978-1-897475-44-7
— Deborah Panko – Cobourg – *Somewhat Elsewhere*
  – Poetry – ISBN – 978-1-897475-13-3

Forth set of five books

— Diane Dawber – Bath – *Driving, Braking and Getting out to Walk*
  – Poetry – ISBN – 978-1-897475-40-9
— Patrick Gray – Port Hope – *This Grace of Light*
  – Poetry – ISBN – 978-1-897475-34-8
— John Pigeau – Kingston – *The Nothing Waltz*
  – Prose – ISBN – 978-1-897475-37-9
— Mike Johnston – Cobourg – *Reflections Around the Sun*
  – Poetry – ISBN – 978-1-897475-38-6
— Kathryn MacDonald – Shannonville – *Calla & Édourd*
  – Prose – ISBN – 978-1-897475-39-3

Fifth set of three books

— Tara Kainer – Kingston – *When I Think On Your Lives*
  – Poetry – ISBN – 978-1-897475-68-3
— Morgan Wade – Kingston – *The Last Stoic*
  – Novel – ISBN – 978-1-897475-63-8
— Kathryn MacDonald – Shannonville – *A Breeze You Whisper*
  – Poetry – ISBN – 978-1-897475-66-9

Sixth set of three books

— Bruce Kauffman – Kingston – *The Texture of Days, in Ash and Leaf*
  – Poetry – ISBN - 978-1-897475-86-7
— Chris Faiers – Marmora – *Eel Pie Island Dharma: A hippie memoir/haibun*
  – A memoir in haibun form – ISBN - 978-1-897475-92-8
— Theodore Michael Christou – Kingston – *an overbearing eye*
  – Poetry – ISBN – 978-1-897475-93-5

Seventh set of four books

— Alyssa Cooper – Kingston – *Cold Breath of Life*
  – Poetry – ISBN – 978-1-927725-02-3
— Bruce Kauffman – Kingston – *The Silence Before the Whisper Comes*
  – Poetry – ISBN – 978-1-897475-98-0
— S.E. Richardson – Kingston – *Before I Lose Light*
  – Poetry – ISBN – 978-1-927725-05-4
— G. W. Rasberry – Kingston – *More Naked Than Ever*
  – Poetry – ISBN – 978-1-927725-04-7

Eighth set of six books

— Brian Way – Carrying Place – *redirection*
  – Poetry – ISBN – 978-1-927725-20-7
— David Pratt – Kingston – *Apprehensions of Van Gogh*
  – Poetry – ISBN – 978-1-927725-21-4
— Felicity Sidnell Reid – Colborne – *Alone*
  – Young Adult Novel – ISBN - 978-1-927725-18-4
— James Ronson – Port Hope – *Power and Possessions*
  – Novel – ISBN – 978-1-927725-22-1
— Morgan Wade – Kingston – *Bottle and Glass*
  – Novel – ISBN - 978-1-9227-19-1
— Jim Christy – Belleville – *Bad Day for Ralphie*
  – Short Stories – ISBN - 978-1-927725-23-8

www.ingramcontent.com/pod-product-compliance
Lightning Source LLC
LaVergne TN
LVHW040153080526
838202LV00042B/3145